I0333981

Boomerang Code

By Peter Koren

ISBN: 978-1-0670653-0-0

2025 Edition
Paperback

Derived from a series of released articles and excerpts from the book *"Seeing Beyond 2020 Vision"* by Peter Koren.
We are cooking some riddles and puzzles in the alphabet soup that's been brewing since 2020.

Published by GLOWING LIGHT LTD
Auckland New Zealand

2025 Edition has New Cover and illustration added.
Slight change to Title *"The"* removed.

20 20

2020 2021 2022

^ ^

0 0

V

_____/

20 21 22

Table of Contents

Riddles Resolve

This book is a collection of riddles, puzzles and strange sayings about the strange puzzling events beginning 2020, with some ozzie slangs, jingle jangled in around them.

You know like just throwing it out there and seeing what comes back!

These sayings are guaranteed to spin you around.
If you can make head and tail out of them then you are true blue sport.
Well they say if you cant beat them join them, they have thrown us some whoppas these last couple of years and if you are going blind trying to work it out, then blame the science.

Random riddles require resolve.

Here is some riddles that would make The Riddler proud, *Batman and Batwoman.*

What is round but also barbed and gets in where nothing should?

Unique inserts spike pattern, gain of function Sars Mers Corona cocktail mix, a gain of entry host hack, with retro viruses lurking our immune response is on fire!
Who is responsible or is something behind the who? Bats soup stirred in the lab going viral onto the world, they patented it, they published it, peer reviewed it, still alluded it, the scientific godfathers knew what was in the brew, locked up society composed a solution, inserted and tattooed tracking the DNA infused,
the drones are watching all,
temperatures are rising, don't worry we got masks and not shaking the hands anymore, antibodies anti our body deadly strain the brain, you got this figured out where it came from?

M

Muse Me M
Modifications Mayhem Messing Munity
Manipulation Mouse Mutations Medications
Malignant Models Murder Mystery Mortality
Mint More Money Missing Millions
Making Monitored Masses Misery
Malicious Managing Mad Men
Mafia Militia Mercenaries Mobsters
Mayhem Mounted Madness
Megalomaniac MisManaged Municipalities
Mirrored Maligned Messed Movements
Most Modernism Morons Maulings
Matter Mutter Mental Minions Marauders
Missing Mark Masked Monster
Mocking Minds Manipulating Masses Media
Meddling Mentioned Material
Minced Measured Mixed Messages
Missing Messing Muzzling
Mad Mad Mad Master Movie
Monumental Marxism Morose Mao
More Musing Mr Murky Mule
Me Move Mission Manage Miracle
Magnificent Mighty Moses

Another puzzling message from the Riddler, Batman and Batwoman, work it out!

Conspiracy Construct Composite
Covert contemptible culpable coalition conglomerates
Cagey camouflaged commie chumps caboodle
Crippling crooked cowards cacophony
Cunning conniving creepy constant cursed coots
Conforming convoluted criminals calamity
Caustic chronic clamour catastrophe
Causes collared convicts colony
Come clear converted

Infected Golf Balls

This is a Covid Alert about the spread of a fatal pandemic by a deadly infected golf ball.
Did you know that if you play golf there is a high risk that you could kill someone with the virus.
That's right, we are basing this on strong scientific evidence using golf ball projection models from super computers, as well as advice from experts in disease transmission by projectiles, our findings clearly show that the virus can become air borne forming a viral cloud when blasted into the air by a whopping slog by these irresponsible golfers.

This is a serious threat that we are facing right now to our state and wellbeing, which is the possibility of being struck by a stray or targeted infected golf ball.
This is due to some irresponsible and sometimes enraged golf players engaging in this illegal activity.
This is particularly disturbing at this time during a pandemic as the golf balls have been shown to increase the spread of the virus.
The following is information and the background into what led up to this growing threat to society and the effects of the golf ball infection, infection numbers, including a scientific detailed explanation of how this phenomenon occurs linked to the spike protrusion of the golf ball.

This is going on right now, the state that we are in is terrible and we need to take action immediately before things get way out of control.

It has been revealed through intensive analysis that the spike protrusion of the golf ball has been enhanced in golf balls manufactured and enhanced in a specialised lab with a gain of function ability.

The virus will also gather on the spike protrusion and when struck with particular aggression by the perpetrators will create airborne virus clouds that are increasing the spread over large regions where the golf balls have been struck by the unlawful activities of these alleged offenders.

Read on you just won't believe it, it could not be true surely but yes things are that bad.

Therefore if you live within 5 km from a golf course you maybe at risk of catching the covid from enraged crazed rogue golfers protesting the enforced rules and out to prove a point. These crazed individuals without a care for anyone else other than their own handicap, will stop at nothing to drive their point home. The good news is that they only can play the game in daylight and we know for a scientific fact that the virus is only active after 8pm or in the case of daylight savings it will make the calendar adjustment to 9pm.

So this means unless they play under powerful night lights and risk a huge fine and being spotted and chased down tackled to the ground by some law enforcement militia in combat uniform.

Therefore you will have minimal chance of catching the virus from a loose golf ball smacked into your vicinity, breathe a sigh of relief and say a hoorah for our chief and commander comrade Dan for all of his careful attention to the critical details to combat this virus.

These inquiries looking into our handling of this deadly pandemic and criticisms from the odd alternative media are just a lot of fuss most likely driven by these fringe conspiracy closet golfers that have no real appreciation of elimination strategies, don't they know that sensible managed minimising and prevention is not enough, we need to get tough and blow the stupid economy to kingdom come if need be and forget about peoples mental health, we can keep throwing federal money at the economy anyway and besides we are all crazy here so what difference will it make if we are driven more crazy.

I am so glad that there are places in this world where we crack down on irresponsible people. Thankyou Dan and from the hash tag support Dan Brigade.

We all just need to say you are my hero, you have saved us from well who knows what something bigger that what I can think about and you put Victoria on the road map, ride the North East link into the red sunset, forget the trams take the chinese train. Victoria is world famous and Melbourne is such a strong city unless you are a business owner, well you can all buzz off, complainers, what is this being financially secure, we got handouts to Africa just line up.

Take control Dan, take control of the silly masses, just subjects what do they know they need your leadership, do the thinking for them take away resistance it is futile, the borg hive mind got the right idea.

Just get the jab, stop whining won't hurt puts a tracker in you better surveillance, we will know when you cross the red line over 5km, you crooked criminals.

Dan's leadership style reminds me of a movie called cable guy.
"What you have done is highly illegal, you will be fined $5000 and sent off to a state penitentiary."
"I could be your best friend or your worst enemy." quotes from the movie Cable Guy. Dan will know if you are his friend by the secret handshake test.

By complying to the rules we have just made one more sensible step towards elimination. Elimination of what???
It will be all worth it, no stray golf ball will come anywhere near your household and infect you, danger danger Dan Da Man warning warning.

News Flash!!! Virus mutated from night time infection to 24 hours infection, the virus has had an update and a patch to operate easily 24 hours and therefore, the curfews are no longer of any use to management.

If these criminal golfers want to inflict injury on the innocent public, who are basically sitting ducks and will be picked off one by one by some infected golf balls projected in their general direction, remember the air borne molecular particles of this virus has a long range and can be like a cluster bomb effect on its victims covering a broad metropolitan area, so don't try running although you should be wearing a mask which offers massive protection over the whole of your mouth area, possibly an umbrella will also offer some protection as well, this has not been fully tested as we do not have many willing volunteers, but we may be able to trial this on the general public for the common good of all since the virus itself is mainly a social experiment so why not!!!

The other fortunate thing is that we have kept the 5km rule in place and this should restrict the golfers from accessing golf courses, but of cause we are very generous with the public as they can now go on nature walks in the national parks and get much needed fresh air and exercise if they have a national park within 5kms of their residence, you know if you stray from this there will be a $5000 fine.

Completely justified, I don't care if you are in the Simpson desert we will get you and you may infect the explorers in the desert like burke and wills you selfish thing you!

Even if the golfers use their own mini golf course and send projectiles of which some are believed to be directed at parliament house they have no appreciation of all our hard work, we have devised new legislation for some of our trained public servant thugs militia brigade, maybe a few spare underground CCP officers could be handy to arrest these golfers and if they suspect that you are even thinking of doing these crimes they also have the power to detain you indefinitely, a menace to society must be removed, we need conforming programmed indoctrinated happy people to be part of our overall program and all will run smooth and be happy, no golfers permitted in the new normal, we will send you to special retraining camps to be model citizens of our brave new ordered strong city world.

We also have an idea who the possible ring leader of these resistance group of golfers is, none other than the former AFL Star, angry at us for no apparent reason, we just can't recall any reason, yes he is none other than Sammie Snapper. Dan says we are on to him we got the surveillance, drones are on to him, he thinks he got away with it but we know what he is up to, we know that he purchased large quantities of golf balls on ebay,

ha ha we are too good, noone escapes our ever watching eye, that is you know that eye in the pyramid thing, I think Dan can go all the way to the top of this pyramid thingy the way he is going.

Whoops there is another tin foil hat wearing former AFL player whistle blowing conspiracy person warning about corruption and all sorts of hidden things, how did Gary Ace know? Did he get inside our thinktank, he doesn't know the handshake does he?

This golfing activity is now getting out of hand and then there is also the people going to a beach on a beautiful hot spring day, what do I say, "oh golly gosh gee wizz, just stay home and follow the rules why don't you and I don't recall any reason why you must do that except that those are the rules. Dan Da Man he got a handicap 666.

If you are thinking of leaving our state, great all part of the plan, our strong city will be populated by model citizens from the globalist population, this is the super city, super strong city utopia we have rules in place like no other except maybe our sister cities with our mates Kim and Xi.
Remember I can be your best friend or your worst enemy. Elimination of the nasty virus called *"Victoria in the lucky country of the free"*, is the plan.

Super Spreader Shepparton.

Shepparton is a City in Victoria where a Covid 19 infected truckie escaped from the wall of steel surrounding Melbourne the capital of Victoria in the severest lockdown, spreading virus havoc on this Victorian City. You know the story in country Victoria where there has been minimal cases very few deaths, but still subject to harsh lockdowns. This truckie made the news with his super spread, when he got out while infected by the virus into unsuspecting country Victoria, which if proper tracing was used like NSW and just about anywhere in a western country could have minimised the spread. Just about all of Shepparton panicked after finding out he had visited McDonalds and other spots on his rampage, fear then kicked in fuelled by the media. Lets all rush in and be tested by improper unreliable tests, Dan how could this happen you had the virus all locked up?

What a farce and big hoax we live in, repeated advice, yes the virus exists take precautions, HCQ oh yeh that is a cure that is banned, OK other helpful immune boosters like a lemon, then protect the vulnerable and we will survive this pandemic flu without killing our economies. Suckers. Well I am actually livid about all this destruction, I went to school in Shepparton grew up there, know the place well. So the Super Spreader in Shepparton did what? Really!!!

Symbolic Race the Americas Cup

How about this one people, patriots? Those who are asking hard questions, those wanting answers and those who are not sure, confused, flipping one way then another.

The Americas Cup was traditionally dominated by USA since its beginnings in 1851
until recently when firstly Australia won it dramatically for the first time in 1983.
Now New Zealand have got into the act and are the reigning champs of this prestigious yacht race.

Notice how New Zealand have been praised for handling the COVID Pandemic and are the model Nation for others to follow.
This has been the challenge for western countries managing this pandemic which is debatable whether it is a genuine pandemic or is it a Positive PCR done over 24 Cycles Test pandemic? *(reader do some research on recommended 24 cycles increased to 40 cycles used for the PCR Test)*

Question is while managing the pandemic what is the effect on western economies and is there certain nations and some in the elite billionaire class that are benefiting from this economic hit while the rest suffer?

Now looking at the most recent race on the 30th Jan 2021 in New Zealand we have USA v Italy.

In the races leading up to this concluding race the American yacht had been plagued with technical issues from day one where it sped to the lead as expected but then suddenly the boat flipped over on the turn in the first race and from there it was game over.

Does this sound familiar? November 3rd a certain event happened where results flipped over causing the other challenger to win. Since then the America Yacht has been crippled and unable to get back in the lead.

Now to top off this result we have the final race where America had to win to keep its chances alive on the 30th Jan.
In the first race on this day USA came pretty close with no mishaps but still not enough to pass the challenger.

Then came this final race where this could have been declared a draw keeping hopes alive if America won sending things into the tie breaker with extra races to name a winner. What happened however was a major hit to the yachts remaining hopes, this time there was a bug in the computer system disabling the yachts abilities and it lost the race convincingly unable to regain control due to this major technical hitch in the system.

This is a symbolic event with a reference to the actual event. Not saying the Italian crew somehow disabled the American yacht and the result will be turned by the judges, no that one is done all above board and happened symbolically to point to an actual event where things were dodgy.

If we research the real news. it happens that Italy did it! and all roads lead to Rome, as in the American Embassy in Rome where a collusion of countries with an agenda had Operatives with highly specialised computer manipulation capabilities switched a ton of data from the already questionable Voting Software Systems which are connected to the internet through a back door by using military grade encryption with the Leonardo satellite system to cover up this major manipulation, turned the result around, flipped it, draw your own conclusions.

Join the dots, see the connections, no joke it happened, what do you think will happen now? Justice will strike the hammer blow!

Rhyme and a Reason

Pop goes the weasel!

The sound of the weasel popping off will be heard loud and clear in and out the eagle, as soon as the monkey stopped to pull up his sock, pop goes the weasel!
The whistleblowers will be popping off, it is happening already and has been intensifying, but now it is headed for Krakatoa, a massive unstoppable historic eruption with worldwide consequences!

Whistleblowers can be a very significant personnel and what they say will not be able to be refuted or denied and swept under the carpet.
There are ways and means to get the information simultaneously and continually to the government agencies, authorities, mainstream and alternative media, social media and all of the filters will not be able to stop it!
Once the big one happens, a lot more will come out of the woodwork, popping their head out and they won't be the only ones becoming visible to the public, corruption and lies will be exposed with an unprecedented explosive cloud covering the earth, increasing uncontrollable numbers will surface from their caves with security measures in place for their protection.

If those who should take action don't, they will be exposed, due to the spread of information and it is known if they are not compromised they must take action and follow the rule of the law or they are not fulfilling their duty and oath to serve.
Security will be easier because of the overwhelming numbers no longer controlled by big brother, brother you are history!
Time is up! The alarm will sound! Loud and clear, get your house in order or suffer the consequences and too late to cover up, erase and hide the evidence it has already been uncovered and released.
You might be able to run but you can't hide!

I saw someone significant on their laptop releasing information to the strategic targets using smart technology, when you go to capture them they will no longer be there, gone to Timbuktu.
Pop goes the weasel!
Something triggers them and suddenly they will shift from being quiet conforming on side to coming out and sharing all.
I pray for stealth, cloaking and clouds of covering, angels are dispatched for this operation and security over those who will come out to release significant evidence that will turn it all around and shift the current administration of corruption out of practice.

Intercessors if this registers, go to war!
Can you hear the sound of the Mulberry Trees whistling?

"Pop Goes the Weasel"

British version:

Half a pound of tuppenny rice,
Half a pound of treacle.
That's the way the money goes,
Pop! goes the weasel.

Up and down the City road,
In and out the Eagle,
That's the way the money goes,
Pop! goes the weasel.

American version:

All around the Mulberry Bush,
The monkey chased the weasel.
The monkey stopped to pull up his sock,
Pop! goes the weasel.

Half a pound of tuppenny rice,
Half a pound of treacle.
Mix it up and make it nice,
Pop! goes the weasel.

18th Century Nursey Rhyme

It's happening brothers and sisters.

Give God all the Praise and Glory, He is revealing hidden things to His servants and nothing is too hard for Him to change in a flash!

Are you in agreement? Are you for us or against us? God is for us!
The knowledge of the Glory of the Lord will cover the earth, nothing can stop the coming billion plus harvest.
Gods heart is none should perish and all should come to the knowledge of salvation and we all got our part as coheirs partnering with Him.

Choose Life!

Hickory, Dickory Dock!

Any idea what time it is?

We have been taught as children to read the time.
Other signs then alert us to that time.
The mouse is running up the clock and we know that something is up when the time approaches.
The Clock strikes one and we have arrived, it is past midnight, or is it high noon?
The mouse is alarmed and runs back down.
The mouse can no longer hide, the mouse was getting up to some things, then when that clock strikes, suddenly bingo down he goes in plain sight to all!

The Hickory is being pounded out, flowing like milk and honey, we had to pound this thing, we didn't leave it alone as we would have no cream.

The Dock with the long taproot. When we tried to pull it out only the top came off, but the deep rooted thing stuck around like a noxious weed.
Well when this one finally gets pulled out, we are going to get our tonic and healing after the nation being stung.
When we were young and free we were taught to tell the time, we used to hear that sound, could see the mouse going up and down.
Don't you go believing the lying rhymers now, they package it well, sweetened up media treats, just a cheap trick clock, don't buy into it or you will lose the telling time just right.

Tick tock, tick tock!

Hickory Dickory Dock!
The mouse ran up the clock.
The thief came a lying, stealin, cheatin in the night.
The clock struck one.
The mouse came down.
Hickory Dickory Clock!
The clock will strike and you can't shift the times and seasons we are in.
Now the clock will strike, hence the return of the Trump Card.

Hickory Dickory Dock

Hickory dickory dock
The mouse ran up the clock
The clock struck one
The mouse ran down
Hickory dickory dock

English Nursery Rhyme 1744

Charismatic celebrities and cunning spin doctors are employed to weave self-righteous thinking and lies covered and sweetened by pretentious values and promises and tales of equality and equity.

They are the blind teachers of falsehood and blind guides leading the blind into the pit of doom. What they say and espouse appears to be valid and are convincing to the ones without discernment to see the underlying dark philosophies that have the agenda to replace God with a false god and make us all a god of our own utopias, they use the algorithms and filters of mind control to suppress the truth and only present their lies, but these bubbles will burst as they do not have true substance and can hold nothing.

The so called wisdom of this world will be destroyed by the Light of truth exposing all of the dark satanic lies and the so called wisdom that controls our media and airwaves -

- infiltrating the thinking of men and women unaware of the danger and corruption effecting them by taking it in as truth, the wisdom that comes from below is demonic in origin and can't be trusted, it has the power to twist pervert and spin great deception on those who allow these lies to take root in their minds taking them down the pathways of destruction and being useful idiots for the enemy opposing the truth.

Lies, lies and more lies will be exposed on an unprecedented and earth shattering Richter Scale.

The Truth will be revealed.
Justice will be served that will leave no stone unturned, documents, evidence of massive deep state rooted corruption will be revealed and the strong arm of the rule of law will act to bring convictions, indictments, with compensation and damages restored.

Those involved in crimes against humanity and treason who are corrupt members of Government, Judiciary and Media who work for their own pockets and do the bidding for dark entities that have an agenda to control and enslave humanity will be convicted for their crimes and overthrown from their positions of power and influence, swept aside by the shaking and sweeping reforms, swiftly bringing justice with no place to hide!

See how they run, see how they run, three blind mice, three blind mice, the corrupt members of Government, Judiciary and Media, three blind mice, three blind mice, their tales got chopped off, did you ever see such a sight?

Jack Be Nimble

Jack be nimble,
Jack be quick,
Jack jump over
The candlestick.

English Nursery Rhyme 1815

Certain Nursery Rhymes are known to have a dark twist to their seemingly harmless fun story and it is a disturbing thing that these kids' kindergarten stories are presented to children with young tender minds to learn about.
Let's look at Disney, harmless entertainment for the family focus on the kiddies, tune into the Mk Ultra training Program for young aspiring actors.
The Media controls your airwaves, your thoughts and what your children will believe.
It is now overturned, reversed and all that was stolen will be restored to those under this enslavement by the dark entities corrupting the planet, we need to turn our trust in the Lord and not lean on our own devices and the strength and power of Pharaoh and the gods of Egypt.

The tables are turned in the favour of justice, all the lies will be exposed, the thieves will be apprehended and tried and what was stolen will be put back in place.
The thief comes to steal, kill and destroy.
The thief does not enter through the door which is Christ Jesus, He comes through an illegitimate way.
The thief steals what is intended for good and corrupts the gifts to be used for his evil plans.
The sheep do not listen to the voice of the stranger, they follow the Shepherd and know His voice is the truth and the Shepherd loves His own and cares for them.
Jesus came that we might have life and life in abundance.

The candle stick delusion.
This rhyme was written with the intention that the ability to leap over a candlestick is as if like magik that Jack was specially empowered to defy the common laws.
But now as this is the time of a great reset which is not the planned great reset but one that is divinely orchestrated where the powers used by corrupt individuals are overthrown.
Things that seem to gain control and get away with all sorts of atrocities to mankind will be judged and tried and the outcome will be reversed!
They are thieves and robbers coming through the illegal door, gaining power from the dark to pull off their sinister schemes and trick the world that this is how things are done.

Behind the secret closed doors will be ripped open and the world will see into this mess and totally abhor it, no longer be subject to it. Those that involve the dark arts and employ tricks to defy the laws will not be able to get away with it any longer as their candle lit power will be extinguished.
Instead the candle of justice will burn all those depending on their magik to leap over the light unscathed and will instead suffer the consequences from the searing heat of the candle of justice.

The Ports and Hotels getting busted in a clean-up operation. A street sweeper will go through cleaning up the traffik and unblocking the truth all about Evergreen Street. The ever smart will be out smarted and container contents will be tipped up.

Weiner gate laptop withdrawn from sale when the videos leaked out. Islands are shaking, their temples falling down, their candle cooked up spirits coming down in cuffs into town, Johnny and company, Isaac saw you and ran up the street pursued, he never did come back and talked no more.

Running rings eating pizza in the networks, Jack be quick the law is coming, Jack be nimble, the judges will no longer play your tune, Jack got fried by the heat of the candlestick.

I hear a true sound coming out of the Wood, whistles blowing in the wind, it is all coming out now and it will rattle the foundations of DC to New York, New York. Revealing winds are blowing stripping it all bare in Georgia, in the deserts of Arizona, all the way through Highway 62 to sunny California will howl, even in Death Valley the Navajo stand up and take notice.

The spirit of man is the candle of the Lord and God will shine a bright burning light on hidden acts of darkness where corruption will be exposed for all to see, no more flying over the radar undetected you have been inspected, tick tock and found wanting.

What worked in the past cloaked in a sinister cloud will feel the flame and fall from the sky with those leaping into this magik come falling down like crazed meteors burning in spectacular fashion for the world to see.

Jack will be caught up in his web of deceit at the height of his leap, the web that was spun to deceive, where sick things are permitted to operate with a blind eye and looking the other way, no questions were asked by the compromised all the way up to the supreme.

Remember with all of the counterfeit gifts there is the true and so it is with Jack.

The prayers and the righteous decrees of the saints have been heard in the Heavenly Court, justice justice, favour favour, the gavel has fallen overturning the dark modus operandi and now the tables are turned.
The rule of law will be applied and the thief caught and will pay for the damages and this will reverse the devastation and what was previously allowed by corrupt rulers to continue without penalty.

Now is the time for the true iconoclastic to arise, these ones are not lawless, they are operating in the spirit of the law, which is the law of the spirit of life where there is grace and protection by the blood of Jesus in the Passover and they have great freedom to perform leaping signs and wonders that will dazzle the whole earth.
A billion souls plus is at stake and this is the awakening and the reason why this all must be reversed, a reverse of the curse, stars for scars, a unprecedented wealth transfer on the way and can't be stopped, it is a glory freight train full of abundance of blessings and wealth. The Kingdom of God is advancing full steam ahead.

Nothing can stop it, neither death, nor life, nor angels, nor principalities, nor powers, nor things present, nor things to come, nor height, nor depth, nor any other creature can stop the power of love.

Let's turn this thing around for good, Jack the black is saved and delivered, now he is a new creation the old is passed away, Jack in the white light and Jill are saved and delivered they are new creations and the old is history.

Now Jack is true nimble and Jack is true quick, he is now in the light, the only way he cannot disrupt the light on the candlestick is when he is in sync with the light source.
The candle of man is light of the Lord.
Jesus lights up mankind and He is the light of life.
Harmony and flow will anoint you to move with ease through the challenging and the impossible, you will have the freedom to leap like never before witnessed like an iconoclastic Jack turbo charged.

Jack may have a reputation of a dark pirate running from the law, but underneath this skilful character is an individual breaking the mould, not bound by the status quo of conforming to the pattern of mediocrity and the cookie cut woke, saying the same, thinking like the same old parrot taught what to say and think, not how to think!
There is an attitude and a freedom that does not conform to the ways of the world keeping those earthbound, tied down to the constraints imposed by the globalist laws and doctrines of worldly thinking and rules that are pointless imposed by the police states of irrational government control.

God doesn't want us to be fashioned into programmed DNA robots all thinking and saying the same old spouting nonsense.

Iconoclastic Jack.
Gifts are excelling in favour released.
Jack are the elusive fellows with a kind of out of the box reputation, not fitting in to the contrived new norm and conforming by the rules, a mischief to the authorities, he seems to evade capture and is admired by those who can't get out of this box.

When Jesus came He had this type of reputation and the religious authorities despised Him, He wasn't contained and when He moved and spoke it was pure talent and a delight to behold.
He shook society to the core, challenged the norms and He walked on water, you couldn't keep this man down.
The news reported Him, but He didn't say what they wanted and do what they wanted, He was unpredictable impossible to trap, He was above and beyond, He saw above and beyond any 2020. Jesus was walking and talking freedom.

Jesus was the true iconoclastic and we are conformed into His image, do you think that means we all dress the same, look the same, talk the same, say the same arguments lined up like ducks in a row, clowns with open mouths waiting for our next thinking pill and a jab for our DNA alteration? Think again!

He has created us all unique with gifts and callings set apart from others to contribute something new, complimentary and helps support others, filling up the missing pieces lacking in our society and progressing us into completeness in the image of the Head of this Body of believers, Jesus our Lord and Saviour who is the teacher for free thinkers and liberty.
Free your mind!
If the Son sets you free you are free indeed.

Born again and saved, free spirited Jack and Jill are going up the mountain.
Jack won't fall down and he will retain his crown.
A peculiar people, Kings and Priests ruling and reigning. The real trick is not to focus on the problem, which is all of the corruption and the evil practices that is going on in this fallen world.
We need to focus on the solution.
The solution is Jesus Christ came to set us free from our evil ways and give us a new life.
Jesus is the door into freedom where all things are possible, be nimble and be quickened.
Christ in us is the hope of Glory.
We are the righteousness of God in Him and we are a new creation the old has gone and the new has come.
Harvest time is here for Jack and Jill.

Happy Easter Resurrection Sunday.

Peace on earth.

The previous chapters are mostly excerpts taken from my previous book entitled "Seeing Beyond 2020 Vision".

Just throwing a few wobblies, spinning some yarns with you cobbers!
The following Chapters are like a flow on, just keeping the ball rolling and really going down the creek in a barb wired canoe mate.

True Blue News for You

This is Australia Victoria where I was born, no longer the place I grew up in, the lucky country she'll be right mate!
Democracy no more.
Totalitarian prison for convicts, lock up your citizens, fine them unless they be quiet take a shot in the arm and say nothing.
You got galahs all in a row being shot left right and centre still going to get yu!
Ned Kelly wore a tin can mask would you lock him up if he took it off cause he had to smoke a ciggie?
Dan's got all the answers until you ask him about the corruption, then he doesn't recall anything.

Oi Oi Ozzie! Ozzie the place where you follow the science.
If the footy gets kicked into the crowd, scatter you can't let the footy touch you, it's got the footy flu and its gonna kill yu! By order of the health minister in SA (Sucker Aussie).
You can play golf but if you need to pee you can't use the dunny and the police made sure by locking all of the loos on every golf course in Melbourne the super lockup city.

Oi Oi Ozzie!
We will open up when we get zero, you'll get zero when everyone is deceased from the lockups.

We got a roadmap but it's the longest straight road in the desert of the never never reaching the targets where everyone falls asleep from boredom and crashes.
If you lived in the most locked up city in the world, you would drive on that road beyond the black stump of Bourke any day on the roadmap outa here!

Oi Oi Ozzie!
Follow the science should be follow the money, who's getting paid for what by whom, nudge nudge wink wink a secret handshake or two, a lob here and a lob there fizzer and astrazoolicker, ask the question smell the rat and you will get arrested and hung in Ballarat. The boys in blue have gone black, they will knock you down and pepper you just ask an old lady, they will shoot you and arrest you and fine you and they are doing it for your health.

Oi Oi Ozzie!
Next time get young eistein to do the science, this is blooming ridiculous yahoo seriously knock it off!

Crocodile Dundee and the unmasked croc.
Crocodile Dundee was doing his rounds in the swamp one day.
When he came across a resistant croc without a mask.
Crocodile Dundee thinks I gotta do the right thing and sort out this crook of a croc.

So he confronted him, ordered him to put on your mask.
That flipping croc just snapped back at Dundee what a cheek.
So he wrestled him in the swamp they rolled around and Crocodile Dundee true to form got that mask on him.
Wiped his smerk got a mask on it now.
The big croc just snapped it off in a flash not taking it lying down.
Dundee says I am not having this and took him down rolled around in that swamp in a fury until he got another mask on that big snark of a croc.
Again he just snarled snapped and ripped it off.
Right that's the last straw says Dundee.
I will dob you into the authorities, that's the ozzie thing to do here, so when the croc was looking away, Dundee made the call to the boys in blue they do it for you.
Gotta big fella here he won't take the mask, come here with that tank and the riot squad we will show him who's boss, wrestle him and hold him down and force that mask on that croc, wipe that smerk of his big chops.

Can't have your germs in our swamp you selfish croc.
Crocodile Dundee a fair dinkum ozzie, true blue good bloke for a mate.

The land of the nasties downunder.

We got some of the biggest spiders aplenty, poisonous ones galore.
A red back on the toilet seat quite a nasty one.
Snakes in the grass we got plenty of em lurking out there under a log watch your step empty your sleeping bags.
Even the bluie octupussie will sting yu to death.
We had the sickest buildings around, legionnaires very nasty in the air con could take you down for more than just a sickie.
Not to mention the bush fires all up in smoke hazards to your health.
Big bush flies that bite you, bull ants that give you a nip.
Then we got the big white shark jaws on steroids makes surfing not all that cruisey.
Crocodiles now they got big mouths and snapping jaws you go for a dip and don't make it back to shore.

The land of some real nasties downunder.
Us ozzies just say, she'll be right mate no worries cobber just another day.
Hasn't stopped us getting out before on a hot summers day, any day for that matter.
But now we have the biggest swamp bunyip like never before.
Not just any old flu, a new one made up to top them all, we are running scared now, we are locked in can't go out for this one that's what they say and they would know.

Trust that old stinger ray with our very life,
ouch that hurt, seemed like an okie dokie idea
at the time!
What you don't know won't hurt you, good on
yu mate!
The land of nasties downunder.

God help us all!

Double Speak

The only double speak here is coming out of Dan's mouth, that is he speaks with fork tongue!
truth = lies
wealth = debt
health = poison
peace = war
freedom = slavery
from Dan's textbook 1984 on how to operate a dictatorship and dupe the unsuspecting public under the spell.
Beguile with deceptive speeches the citizens are pampered by the big bro nanny state lets go dan delusion.
Newspeak backs up every word like parroting galahs, they done the handshakes.
Watch your steps, when the truth is revealed and when it all comes out, game over dan, the abuse will cease and justice will be served.
Pride comes before a fall.

Well done all the brave hearts who are awake, making a difference, putting it out there and their voice is heard just watch the real news. This is grass roots not extremists, not told what to think they have done their due diligence, proper research they think for themselves, no longer in the playground of dans kindergarten it's time to grow up, true blue aussies are waking up to the ruse!

Oh OK I get it scomo is being squeezed by hanson and 3 others on his team, now he has to act or face the GG stepping in.

When I put things out there it is to help the wake up process and not to promote fear hopelessness and defeat - it is a call to awake and take action.
We need to magnify the solution not the problem.
Think on good things to bring us into the peace that passes understanding.
Be not overwhelmed with evil overcome evil with good.
Our focus is on the answer.

All of the promises of God are Yes and Amen through Jesus the answer.
He has begun a good work in us and will take us on to completion.
This is not conditional on how bad things look, this is based on faith on our God where all things are possible.
Only believe.

We need to be as wise as serpents and as gentle as doves.
This is Jesus advice when dealing with a corrupt world that uses cunning devices to ensnare its citizens.
So the children of darkness are smarter than the children of light in being street savvy wise, spotting the corruption and the dealer putting one over them.

There is that balance as we need to be as wise as these serpents and know what game they are playing, but we can't strike them like a serpent, we need to remain in love knowing that all have fallen short, so we are as gentle as doves and submit to God resist the enemies devices and God will raise us up in due time. We pray, decree and declare that the unborn and the children, the oppressed and the enslaved will be delivered from the enemies' camp and that justice will be administered, the gates of hell won't prevail and are no match for the host of heaven despatched against them.

You know those armies that surrounded Jerusalem in the ancient days and got obliterated by the armies of heaven, when the mulberry trees rustle and bustle the angels are on the move like the wind you can't see it but it can hit you like a hurricane.
The Glory of God will fill the earth and nothing can stop it, because those forces are below His feet and we are His Body so we are within His feet to trample on snakes and scorpions.

I may not agree with everything that the whistle-blowers, resistance movers and shakers are saying on all of the posts that I have put here and how they tackle the problem we face with control and loss of freedoms, but they are making some things known and exposing the corruption and not bending or conforming to the patterns of this oppressive world.

Do I have all of the answers for each and every case, no way, we are in unprecedented times, we haven't been this way before. One size doesn't fit all.
We all get our own individual paths to follow that fit where we are at and who we are and where we are going and who we will be.
We are created in Christ Jesus for good works, we are His workmanship, He has a plan for each of us to follow.

He knew beforehand what we would be facing and gave each of us a measure of faith, the God kind of faith that moves mountains.
Wait on God, He will renew our strength, we will mount up with wings like eagles and be able to soar above it all.
Submit to God, listen for His leading and instruction, then act accordingly moving forward in faith, one step at a time making sure that we are still on the right path of peace. God is for us who can be against us.

Apparently viruses have an intelligence that will adapt or mutate to find a work around the immune system.

So in let's say about 100 days it will mutate again to counter our defences, this is OK if you rely on natural immunity. However augmented immunity only works to the program within it and then it needs a patch.

Now Pfizzer will come up with a new booster shot to counter the new mutant in 100 days, unfortunately the virus has already counter moved that and mutated again so then Pfizzer will come up with another booster in another 100 days and so on the cycle goes which is great for profits, but very bad for the users.

You are on a merry go round that's moving faster at 100 clicks, click go the shears boys click, click, click.
Click go the shears, boys — click, click, click,
Wide is his blow and his hands move quick,
The ringer looks around and is beaten by a blow,
And curses the old snagger with the bare-bellied yoe.
100 days boys, click, click, click!

"Click Go the Shears" is a traditional Australian bush ballad - 1891

Omicron Transformer

Omicron sounds like a good name for one of the characters from the transformers.

Does that mean that we are being modified by constant program updates inserted into us to end up trans human and end up absorbed into the meta verse like in the movie Tron where we must face a computer programmed creature variant simile and fight against this armoured spiked monster to the death, what happens to you there will affect your material body real time.

Just like the movies some make it out alive, usually the hero and some other main actors, but the rest are just human fodder casualties that are taken out, just how the script goes the insignificant go and the strong remain, Darwin's evolution with some Eugenics thrown in to make sure the quota is achieved in the Gates of Hell.

In the Titan the character played by *Sam Worthington* had to undergo DNA modifications to survive the alien planet, human 2.0 upgrades, some made the program others just crashed out, couldn't breathe under water like a fish so they didn't make the grade.
Some almost make the grade but freak out with extra human strength, go ape and either are taken out or explode.

No one told him that they slipped in the alien code and that there was no going back, it was high risk experimental but necessary for the science and our future existence on planet earth.
Trust the science Frankenstein, because we are the science after all and know what's best for you.

We are only making plans for humans 1.0.
The character Sam Worthington played eventually was assimilated into the alien species where he no longer had empathy for his kind and communicated on a different plane with cosmic frequency shrills, don't mess with him anymore no longer human, no longer only human.

Get the feeling that we are history?
History is being erased no longer applicable in our brave new reset world.
Only problem is God knows the beginning from the end, He knows all that has been and all that will come.
One day we will all have to answer to Him face to face in that courtroom where the most arrogant will be shaking in their boots faced with crimes against humanity and with the evil done in the body and what was done to the body which affects others bodies.
Best to make amends with Him on the way to the Courthouse.
That's a judgement where you are no longer above the law and all is laid bare.

Remember God has made a way.
His kindness leads us to repentance.
The choice is ours to make.
Choose life!

Protestors was how the name for the early Protestants came about during the Reformation.
They protested the institution and controlling church which became the state religion governed by man's dogmas and philosophies on how they see the world which was not based on faith in God.
This sort of attitude taken to the extremes is how we get some self promoting demigods saying I am the science, pride comes before a fall! Doctor Fudgie!

Russian Roulette 1 2 or 3
This is the game of Russian Roulette and there are 3 bullets.
One is a blank, Two will hurt you and Three will kill you.
Even the blanks can kill you if someone isn't careful, someone might switch it around for whatever reason and when you thought you were exempt it backfires against you.
Good luck that's how the game is played, some have to go, some are selected as number one, then others will be allowed to remain, they of cause will be a inferior class fit for the purpose of slave to the new world order system control.

Psycho Riddle

Psycho Cytotoxicity the spike = toxic binds
ACE2 means you are in the stew.
Darpa Karma post Moderna world bio banana tech pfizzer cocktail skull it!
Gene therapy bi polar hyper tension inflammatory response unauthorised for market we are the target!

It doesn't have to end this way.
Save our children. Save our future.
Decree and declare Gods will be done on earth as it is in Heaven.
Speak peace to the storm of chaotic control and destruction.
Take the necessary action to reverse this tyranny before we are sent to the enslavement camps for programming MKUltra style.

There is always Good News.
Where sin abounds grace abounds much more in abundance.
What was meant for our destruction may prove to be the end of a disaster, mild symptoms means natural immunity no need for the jab regime, billions of $ lost billions of people saved fair deal!
When the darkness gets darker the light shines ever brighter.
Jesus is the true light that lights up every one who enters this world.

Grace and Mercy is better than judgement.

For goodness sakes choose Gods offer to embrace you as His child. He created us and knows what is best for us.
God is good. God is love.

Join some scomo dots here blue.

Well you know the constitution says the federal government can't enforce any mandates.
But whoopsie daisy fred! Sorry Ned!
Slipididoodah scomo changed the rules to give the Premiers more power to unleash more supremo controlo over the States.
You know when was that again? Oh round about the time when they could enforce lockdowns for this flipping bat flu bug from the lab arrived through our borders, well that worked out like a ripper for them!
Looks like scomos hands are off the flipping wheel for this one and the premiers enforce the mandates anyway on who? Just your average joe and sheila the citizens of the blooming country where scomo is the head huncho or Mr PM to you blue.

This is like tying the roo down sport, too bad fred its going down like lead!

Oh phone call, gotta go now fred got this call hi my big bro!
Yeh still on track for the bonus me mate!

We got the figures meeting the targets KPIs whatever you want we got the numbers even the kids it all adds up!

We'll make sure to get those ones on walkabout as well in the territory army up there now chasing em down thanks to the gunner.

All good for Christmas,
On the Sixth day of Christmas,
My good friends brought to me some tinsel booster star shining figures in another shipment of shots thankyou el Premiers,
I salute you heil to the hitchler, don't mention the mandates!

There is a spanner in the works.

In NZ Government.

The spanner is the one that turns the cogs which put the wheels in motion.
Now the spanner is synchronising in another revolution of a different gearing upwards.
When the spanner crashes into the cogs sparks will fly, breakdown alarms tripped it will attempt to stop the works before too much damage!
What a blow! Cannot be repaired beyond repair enmeshed mish mashed.
The spanner is in the works and crashed it!

Djokovic No 1 tennis player in the world finds himself in a kangaroo court. He will need more than an ace or two to win this one.
(The kangaroo court refers to the Globalist Agenda Courts playing their game in Australia, not the local court in Victoria, that judge actually was reasonable and fair)

Congratulations!
Novak Djokovic he has shown the world he has a lot more than a couple of aces, he has what it takes - true grit fortitude and character and endurance against the odds.
How will big bro react? Either way even if Big Bro crushes the resistance of a Titan they will look more like the big ugly ogre.

The truth will be revealed and lies exposed. It is funny that when someone who really knows how to play the game also knows the game that is being played by big brother *governpharmatechnocraticment* system of control and this one is powerful enough not to be played by the system, they will usually come across as defiant and showing contempt. *"Hey stop that you are being too loud, we are lining up here in the trance following our pied piper and you are disturbing us!"*

Big brother has the wool over the eyes, but then this rebel comes along and ruffles it all, he shakes the can and all of the worms come falling out for the unsuspecting and the ones being played to see.

"Hush hush don't rock the boat, it's all going to plan unless someone has more than an ace or two."

You have got to hand it to Dan, well played, he saw it coming, good old shifty Dan handled this like a smooth glove.
No 1 Tennis player coming to the State of Victoria unvaxxed with exemption that would rarely be accepted.
Just place the middle man organisation out there to deal with it initially as they want No 1 Tennis Player in the competition, think $$$ in the till and good for the game overall.
Hope that the public and media are diverted by the game and not the exemption.
Lots of red tape spun all around it tangle it up like a good mess.
Between a rock and a very hard place.

Then the mastermind manoeuvre - Dan hands responsibility over to Scomo.
Who is going to look like the big ogre on the world and national stage? Not Dan, well not this time, this is a one big hot potatoe you don't want coming back into your lap.
Smooth and experienced political operator Dan, diverted the blame like a true Public Service employee passing the buck, not my department, quote some legislation in the clear, someone else's problem.
If he was playing doubles, he would slip back and allow his partner to face the grand slam shot coming at him at the net.

Well you lost that one big.
Scomo is wearing this one. That's what a good rally is, passed the ball back over unplayable. Either way he goes it is a win then loss or just a loss.

On the other hand Scomo might still have an ace up his sleeve and sees this as a politically expedient move.
Big Bro the protective one my subjects, I did it for your health, knock the cocky non conformists out of play.
Which way does it go?
Either way time will tell more of the story.
We all got our manoeuvring motives, some good and some bad and some very ugly.

Remember Gallipoli!

The ANZACS.
What do you do with the brave?
They threw us under the bus!

Put our troops on the frontline with machine guns and sharp bayonets pointed at us when we are out in the open, like sitting ducks and can't really see what the enemy is planning! Slaughter house.

Troops are sacrificed for the collective supposed good.

The agenda at all costs where lives are used as fodder and disposed of as inconvenient?

Like lambs to the slaughter in a goat's world.

Well now it's time for operation awakening.

Dead bones alive and kicking back.

My boomerang will come back.

We pray for the situation in Ukraine to minimise, bring resolve, solutions and justice for the loss of life, harm and displacement on the citizens caught up in this as the big boys play war games and monopoly on the big board involving billions and millions.

Oligarchs want to rule at all costs to you!

Warmongers, Oligarchs, shadow boxing elitist rulers overshadowing puppets playing dice with manipulated data and the DNA of souls.

Conspire away, the rats have come out to play and they don't care who gets wiped out on the chess board, while the agenda rolls out on top of people.

Like a rolling stone the millstone will roll back on them as they abused the innocents. Justice is served, time will tell!

The Boomerang Code!

20 20

2020 2021 2022

^ ^

0 0

V

_/

20 21 22

This is about the boomerang effect of 2022. In the visual representation of the code the eyes and the mouth are the instruments of the code.

When the instruments are implemented it will be projected into the atmosphere and it will become like a boomerang effect.
What you put out there comes back to you one way or another for good or bad, a hit in the back of the head or bringing in a favourable outcome.
The eyes involve what your input is, this is what you are allowing through the gateways. Your mind which originally was a clean slate in innocence is being programmed by the information media highway which is your environment, are you able to manage this?

Do you have a filter?
Can you discern what shall be permitted to write upon the tablet of your mind?
Input and output, what comes in will go back out as your expression, what you put inside or allow in, how you hear and what you are seeing is also what you put back out there.
Impressions on the mind; what we believe is the shape of things to come, shaping what we speak thrown out there into the waters of the world.
The waters are like channels, ebbing and flowing with the tide, like carriers of different receptors and amplifiers relaying what is spoken forth.
Channels broadcast like radio station or the media, to be absorbed by the listeners, if there is visuals then this will reinforce an image into the hearts and minds.

2020 eyes

Have the God kind of faith, it is possible for our vision to be heightened above the waters or the prevailing currents, we must heed the warnings, watch out for red flags, get proper advice and stay within the boundaries otherwise the rip tide will drag us under. We can be challenged by the intensity of the waves, it can be hard to focus, the eyes can become blurry and play tricks on us and we may even see illusions. These current prevailing conditions can be overwhelming, unless we take preventive actions to avoid been easily wiped out by the waves.

2022 mouth
Notice the mouth is the shape of a boomerang.
What is being sent out there?
Spinning around and around you can hear the sound of the boomerang in the air above as it penetrates the air creating distinctive waves, it is making a motion and direction to the intended target.
Boomerangs are capable of bringing down small prey, such as bounding wallabies.
Small kangaroos like the young and vulnerable are easy targets.
Will the boomerang sent out coming your way bring in a good return or come back to bite you?

Don't be the problem, be the solution to the problem.

2021 is in between
What we have is the nose and also in the middle are ears on the sides.
What scent are you picking up on? What can you hear is going on?
Do you smell a rat?
The rats are jumping ship!
Its going down water is rising.
No point being loyal and covering up any longer, the heat is on, time to jump look after no 1.
You know you got trouble when rats are running the show.
Trust them to take and eat your assets.
They ramble they scramble away.

The Boomerang Chronicles.

To be or not to be!
That is the question?
To get the shot or not to get the shot!
What if I don't want the shot?
Feels like I am getting shot!
To be free is to be me!

Psalm 103
6 The LORD executes righteousness
And justice for all who are oppressed.

Ecclesiastes 11
Cast your bread upon the waters,
For you will find it after many days.
2 Give a serving to seven, and also to eight,
For you do not know what evil will be on the earth.
3 If the clouds are full of rain,
They empty themselves upon the earth;
And if a tree falls to the south or the north,
In the place where the tree falls, there it shall lie.
4 He who observes the wind will not sow,
And he who regards the clouds will not reap.
5 As you do not know what is the way of the wind,
Or how the bones grow in the womb of her who is with child,
So you do not know the works of God who makes everything.

6 In the morning sow your seed,
And in the evening do not withhold your hand;
For you do not know which will prosper,
Either this or that,
Or whether both alike will be good.

Put the good out there expect a good return.

Sow and reap the good of the land, don't sink into the swamp.
The bunyip roams there waiting for who he can devour.

Isaiah 40
3 The voice of one crying in the wilderness:
"Prepare the way of the Lord;
Make straight in the desert
A highway for our God.
4 Every valley shall be exalted
And every mountain and hill brought low;
The crooked places shall be made straight
And the rough places smooth;
5 The glory of the Lord shall be revealed,
And all flesh shall see it together;
For the mouth of the Lord has spoken."

9 O Zion,
You who bring good tidings,
Get up into the high mountain;
O Jerusalem,
You who bring good tidings,
Lift up your voice with strength,
Lift it up, be not afraid;
Say to the cities of Judah, "Behold your God!"

27 Why do you say, O Jacob,
And speak, O Israel:
"My way is hidden from the Lord,
And my just claim is passed over by my God"?
28 Have you not known?
Have you not heard?
The everlasting God, the Lord,
The Creator of the ends of the earth,
Neither faints nor is weary.
His understanding is unsearchable.
29 He gives power to the weak,
And to those who have no might He increases strength.
30 Even the youths shall faint and be weary,
And the young men shall utterly fall,
31 But those who wait on the Lord
Shall renew their strength;
They shall mount up with wings like eagles,
They shall run and not be weary,
They shall walk and not faint.

Dreams Expansion Revisit.

The following is more from recent dreams discussed on a previous post *https://www.beinginthelight.com/apple.html*

There was a plane a jet airliner in the sky and accompanying the jet was a jet fighter, the airliner falls from the sky suddenly it crashes into a playing field like at a school grounds where you can play sports as well.

A lady gets out wearing a airforce type uniform in white, very smartly dressed, she has very white complexion and looks very sophisticated. She stumbles from the plane and at first walks with some strength like she is OK but then suddenly collapses on the ground next to the crashed plane, she can't get up and walk now in a state of shock and starts to panic as she realises that the plane may explode.
Me and others rush over there to help as well as the other passengers that are still in the plane.

We can see them on board panicking wanting to get out, but appear to be stuck or trapped in their seats for some reason, they look like medical staff in uniform and they are all young men with a similar pale white complexion to the lady who exited the plane.
It seems that the lady is in charge or is the senior officer and the others on board are the foot soldiers rank in training.
Someone says that it is unusual that a jet accompanied this airliner before it crashed.

This is a further interpretation.

I will start with another layer to the interpretation:
The Air Liner and the Pilot as well as the staff represents Government control of a certain country.

The Jet fighter represents foreign control by a dominant force, either a country or a globalist power structure that has control over this Government.
Behind the scene this power is calling the shots or has an overriding influence over the affairs of this country and its citizens by controlling the Government.
The leader or the Captain of the airliner and the staff are all pale in complexion.
This means they are in shock and also have had their life force drained out of them by this power controlling them.

The Puppet show.

Punch and Judy.
He is punch drunk and there is a jolly laughing jester.

Then a further layer to above dream interpretation:

The school grounds may represent the Devils Playground or the field of play for the children of God.

This is where young minds are shaped and at this age they are easily influenced receptors for good or bad.

They can be:

- influenced by peers
- roughed up and bullied
- receive good education or bad education or downright ugly education
- or it can be just playing sports or being entertained on the playing field

It is so easy to end up on the wrong side of things, life manoeuvres, manipulates, mirks you this way and that and you end up flying high, looking smart, not knowing they are playing you. Have compassion on those that fall, even their leaders, you never know who will turn in the end.

I would also like to expand on this dream as well.
I heard in a dream the following - Jacinda said "Ï paid big money to keep them imprisoned" - context New Zealand prime minster.
I sensed however that the guards who are holding the people were actually looking after them and kind towards them.
Now I am in a vehicle which is like a bus on a highway when a crazy looking modern machine vehicle came from the opposite direction to pass by but it somehow entered the bus and I just managed to avoid by moving to the extreme side and it managed to just scrape me without major injury.

There was just like a graze on me where I was seated on this bus that seemed to just open up allowing this vehicle to come through.

This crazy looking vehicle had lots of steel contraptions that are kind of vintage in appearance but also with modern technology, mechanical and steam little pipes with smoke like that movie "Mortal Engines" with machine vehicle wars in a post-apocalyptic modern medieval world.
About that dream I was riding high and cosy in that bus. But then this diabolical machine penetrated the bus and almost took me out! How could the machine enter the bus?

I was seemingly OK in 2019, all was well, yeh maybe I had my issues I was a work in progress, but you know we got time to get through this. Then 2020 hit like a freight train, red pilled left right and centre the rabbit trail just kept going down and down. How could this be? It just isn't time for this scenario! Asleep at the wheel, while the globalist leaders conspired, the machine was already constructed and they pressed the big red button.

What can stop them?
Humans don't always just conform to the plan.

Then there is always the boomerang deployed.

Our seemingly impenetrable place of security.
The walls are breached.
He has something on us.
They are entry points for a very stealth enemy.

Mathew 13
15 For this people's heart is waxed gross, and their ears are dull of hearing, and their eyes they have closed; lest at any time they should see with their eyes and hear with their ears, and should understand with their heart, and should be converted, and I should heal them.
16 But blessed are your eyes, for they see: and your ears, for they hear.

What a wicked web we weave!
The sin that easily entangles us!
The heart is desperately wicked!
O wretched man that I am who can save us?
Thank God for Jesus Christ our Lord and Saviour.

I am crucified with Christ *Gal 2:20*

Or there is another very crafty plot that would lead us to believe that we are doing good works and being good compliant citizens, just obeying orders comrade commander supremo mondo.
However, in reality we are conformed to the patterns of the doctrines of men and devils.
Jesus is our Head and He is Lord, King of kings, all is subject to Him not the other way around.

Religious spirits, deception and false humility.
Colossians 2
18 Let no one cheat you of your reward, taking delight in false humility and worship of angels, intruding into those things which he has not seen, vainly puffed up by his fleshly mind,
19 and not holding fast to the Head, from whom all the body, nourished and knit together by joints and ligaments, grows with the increase that is from God.
20 Therefore, if you died with Christ from the basic principles of the world, why, as though living in the world, do you subject yourselves to regulations-
21 "Do not touch, do not taste, do not handle,"
22 which all concern things which perish with the using-according to the commandments and doctrines of men?
23 These things indeed have an appearance of wisdom in self-imposed religion, false humility, and neglect of the body, but are of no value against the indulgence of the flesh.

The temple needs a good clean out before it can be filled.
There is a requirement for sanctification.
The temple is the focus of the Most High God our Father in Heaven where His will is to be done on earth as it is in Heaven.

How can He achieve this? He needs willing vessels and these vessels need to be sanctified, set apart holy instruments, instruments of righteousness.

Our Temples are the places of authority in the material world to execute righteousness and justice for the oppressed.

We are His mouth and His Hands and feet to do His will on earth, a chosen generation, a peculiar people, His workmanship like new creations that are tuned into the frequencies of Heaven and are on the right wave length to deliver His Kingdom and be carriers of His Glory on earth.

Are we exalted or claiming to be as a god on earth? On the contrary oh religious one, we enter into a paradox, a dichotomy of sorts.

This exchange for the Glory is the humbling thing here as we lay down our lives and take up His life, we cease from our works, enter into His day of rest, His appointed day to be His representatives appealing to the lost to be saved, delivered, set free and then loved and accepted as His beloved in the Kingdom of God where we will live forever with God.

God is our Heavenly Father and Jesus our King and Saviour, with the Holy Spirit filling every cell and our atomic realities to every nano quantum particle. That's why it is crucial what we allow to go into our temples that might alter it, reprogram it, contaminate it, synthesise it corrupt it into a hybrid part human part alien or trans altered species.

Be wise as serpents and gentle as doves, discerning and sensitive to the leading of the Holy Spirit and not swayed by the cunning schemes and false agendas, lying signs and wonders, strong delusions from the patterns of this world governed by the spirit of the air.

Can you see it, even taste it, are you tuned into what God is saying and in agreement, declaring it to be so. What are you sensing, what station are you tuned into?

What motivates you? If the eye is dark then the whole body or temple will be filled with darkness, then the blind guides will lead the blind into the ditch.

Come out and be separate.
Be Holy as He is Holy.

You are bought with a price, your temple is a holy place where God dwells and His will is done as it is in Heaven, where it is already written on your scroll what will be.

Blueprints are drawn up already to perfection, we just need to unroll the plan, learn the keys and the symbols, understanding the workings and how things perform in synchronisation with the Master Plan and then run with it. Ride the horse, your horse is called swift and gallant, you will ride with the wind free.

When Jesus had breakfast on the beach with His disciples. *John 21*
He first of all instructed them to drop the net on the right side.
We are on the left side labouring away in our own strength and wisdom until Jesus shows up shows us the right side and this will bring the return that truly feeds us.

He calls us, reinstates us when we have failed.
Peter feed the sheep.
We are sent where we wouldn't normally go, because we are equipped and accepted warriors for God with faith that He is with us and directs what we say and do and how we influence the atmosphere and others to be loved like we are.

As in the days of Noah.
Noah and the eight were not contaminated by the world and the corrupted humanity to be unredeemable creatures completely lost and swept away by the contrary waves.
Is the insidious plan to abort the man child before he is conceived into existence in the timeline of humanity.
If the gene pool is permanently altered beyond recognition and the corruption is irreversible and then the remaining creatures become trans humanistic zombies, this may put humankind in a continual loop forever lost on planet earth void of any hope, so Christ could never return for His own.

Sounds like a devilish plan that only a globalist elite demi demonic gods would align with to remain here on what remains as earth in a post modern utopia, but in reality is hell on earth on steroids, devoid of God, a paradise for psycho despotic devouring birds to feast on everything that is rotten and decaying matter.

We have read the book and we know how it ends, Armageddon, New Jerusalem, the Bride, the millennial reign. Sorry nasty try, but it is over rover before it even plays out.
The glory train is coming.

Solomon's Temple was filled by the Glory of God and even the priests could not enter.
At that time no flesh or carnality can survive His Presence.
So how do we get there?
The difference is now after the cross and the Resurrection, Jesus became our sin who knew no sin so that in Him we could become the righteousness of God. By faith we are saved and not by our own works and so there is no boasting.

Once we have entered the door we can take one step at a time.
One step of faith at a time.

We grow, we mature, we become like Him, by faith as He is so are we in the world.
This is walking on the water time.

We are positioned above the problem, seated with Him in the Heavenly realms yet being here in bodily form to do His will.
What isn't possible with man is possible with God.
Engaging the spirit that is alive bears good fruit.
He lives so we live also as we are also crucified with Him.
Love God and love others.
Pray in the Spirit.
Have Faith.

Dwell in the Word as He dwelt among us and became flesh and blood identifying with us. Worship in spirit and truth, be in a Relationship with your Heavenly Father so you are a son and daughter knowing what He is doing. Connecting with God like a disciple. Being willing and obedient to His leading.

Make sure you are connected to sound teaching and instruction from those who have gone before us and have demonstrated His power and shown worthy character, clearly they are partakers of the divine nature.

This is a new day, a new awakening, those who have gone before us expect us to go where no one has been before, their ceiling is our floor, we are on the shoulders of giants, what we are facing goes beyond what has been, so we need to go beyond what has been. With God this is possible.

God doesn't use the same old trick over and over, He's got more than we can imagine. Get to know Him as much as possible and He will show you what is possible against all of the odds.

Ask for the solution, don't focus on the problem or speak the problem.
With faith the mountain is removed.
Speak the answer.

Decree and declare a thing and it will be.
If you abide in Him and He in you, ask what you desire and it will be done.

Philippians 2
12 Therefore, my beloved, as you have always obeyed, not as in my presence only, but now much more in my absence, work out your own salvation with fear and trembling;
13 for it is God who works in you both to will and to do for His good pleasure.
14 Do all things without complaining and disputing,
15 that you may become blameless and harmless, children of God without fault in the midst of a crooked and perverse generation, among whom you shine as lights in the world,
16 holding fast the word of life, so that I may rejoice in the day of Christ that I have not run in vain or labored in vain.

Things are already in motion like a Glory Train in full steam.

Get on the right side of the boomerang and the return will bring back the desired harvest.
God's Word doesn't return void but will accomplish His desire and prosper where it was sent.

The ongoing saga of the puzzling riddle!

What if
the very experienced
double agent now in charge
is double crossed?
There is a double jeopardy!!!
When he realises what they have done
set him up
taking them out.

Unnatural deselection.
Eugenics
hierarchy
pyramid scheme.

Only those at the top benefit
the pawns are taken out first
then some knights and bishops
we can sacrifice those
next maybe your castles
ok they might miss those a bit
preserve the queen
keep the king afloat
at all costs.

You can't trust the Schmob.

No honour among thieves
turn for a second knives in the back!

It looks like it is just simple simon and the jester at play.
Look in the right place and you will see it is really a puppet on a string.
The puppet master calls the shots and the fat controller is behind it all.
Look into the shadows and you will find the smooth operator.

The elites connive how to win and influence people.
The world is your oyster.
The pickings are the ID steal.
Carry on up the neo kaizars.
Darkness Kingdom

Not considered by pride and evil.
The higher laws and higher power, justice and right scales.
Also, they underestimated the pawn who made it to the top.
Now a queen bee Esther.
Hangman haman game over.
The ball is back in play for Mordecai.
Kingdom of Light.

BOOMERANG CODE

Acknowledgement of Movie, TV Shows Quotes and references to characters.

There are mostly three recognised Movies TV Shows used for Quotes and characters referenced in a similar style to create a similar narrative, used in this book.

Cable Guy 1996 starring Jim Carrey Columbia and Sony.
Brief quote and similar quote used to make a point.

Batman and Robin TV Series 1966 20th Century Fox.
Mention of the characters Riddler and Batman and Robin, not direct quotes but along the same format of. Then the use of riddles but not the same.

Lost in Space 1965 20th Century Fox.
Mainly The Robots "Warning Warning" and "Danger Danger" quotes.

Boomerang Code

ISBN: 978-1-0670653-0-0

Peter Koren

http://www.beinginthelight.com/

Front Cover artwork and internal images design by Peter Koren

2025 Edition has New Cover and illustration added.

Unless otherwise indicated, Bible quotations are taken from New King James Version of the Bible.

Boomerang Code is available as

978-1-0670653-0-0	Boomerang Code 2025 Edition Paperback
978-1-0670653-1-7	Boomerang Code 2025 Edition Kindle
978-1-0670653-2-4	Boomerang Code 2025 Edition EPUB
978-1-0670653-3-1	Boomerang Code 2025 Edition PDF

BOOMERANG
CODE
2020
2030

www.ingramcontent.com/pod-product-compliance
Lightning Source LLC
Chambersburg PA
CBHW010449010526
44118CB00019B/2519
* 9 7 8 1 0 6 7 0 6 5 3 0 0 *